The Courage of Helen Keller

The sweet scent of honeysuckle floated through the air. The sun was warm. A chickadee hopped along a tree branch, singing. A golden-haired girl, just one year old, sat on a blanket in the grass and looked up at the bird. She laughed at its merry, piping song. Then she looked down at the doll in her lap. She liked its orange woolen hair and button eyes.

"Helen, come to Mama, darling."

The little girl turned around. She saw her mother standing nearby, arms outstretched.

"Ma-ma. Ma-ma," said the child. A smile shining on her face, little Helen stood and toddled to her mother's arms.

5

"Happy birthday!" said Mrs. Keller. "One year old today! Come in and see the presents everyone has brought for you."

The presents looked pretty in their shiny wrappings, but Helen had eyes for just one thing: the birthday cake. It had white icing and pink sugar roses with mint-green leaves. Best of all, it had one tiny candle glowing on top. The flame danced and fluttered. The little girl giggled with delight.

Helen Keller would never see another birthday candle or ever again hear her family sing "Happy Birthday" to her. For when she was one-and-a-half years old, she suffered a terrible sickness. Her fever raged for days. Doctors could do nothing to help her. It was the winter of 1882, and doctors didn't know a lot of things they know now. They also did not have the special medicines called *antibiotics,* which are used today to treat many illnesses. The only thing they could do for Helen was to make her comfortable and pray for her recovery.

Helen did recover, but the illness left her totally blind and deaf. At first, Mr. and Mrs. Keller hoped this nightmare would pass. Mr. Keller would stand near his daughter and clap his hands together sharply. But Helen did not turn toward the sound. Mrs. Keller would hold up an oil lamp. But Helen did not turn toward the light.

Helen's parents finally accepted the sad truth of their daughter's blindness and deafness. But when friends told them that their child was feeble-minded, they could not accept that. They knew that Helen had a bright mind. And they never gave up hope that, one day, she would show the world just how smart she was.

The Kellers did their best to make Helen's life full and happy. They gave her lots of love and attention. They let her roam freely around their home in Tuscumbia, Alabama. She ran through the fields with Belle, the family setter. She rode the small pony that lived in the barn behind the house.

The little girl loved the smell of flowers in the garden, fresh bread baking in the kitchen, and her mother's perfume. She loved the taste of cold ice cream and hot biscuits. And she loved the rough feel of tree bark under her fingertips, and the silkiness of Belle's fur.

There were moments of happiness, like tiny islands in a vast ocean. But mostly, Helen's life was like being alone in a silent, dark room.

Whatever she felt was locked inside. Her love had nowhere to go. Her anger had nowhere to go. Her fears had nowhere to go.

When Helen was five, Mrs. Keller read about a woman named Laura Bridgman, who was also deaf and blind. She had been taught to read and write, and to "talk" to people by using a finger alphabet. Her teacher was Dr. Samuel Gridley Howe, of the Perkins Institute for the Blind, in Boston, Massachusetts.

Laura Bridgman's story gave the Kellers hope that something could be done for Helen. So, as soon as they could, they took her to Baltimore, Maryland, to see an eye specialist. The doctor examined Helen, and said, "I'm sorry, her condition will never change. But she can learn a lot of things. There is nothing wrong with her mind. I have a suggestion to make."

"What is that?" Mrs. Keller asked. "We'll do anything that might help Helen."

"I think you should take her to <u>Washington</u> D.C., to see Dr. Bell. He has had great success teaching deaf people."

The Kellers took a train to the nation's capital. There, they went to see Dr. Alexander Graham Bell. Today, Dr. Bell is remembered mainly as the inventor of the telephone. In those days, however, he was best known for the school he had founded, where teachers were trained to instruct deaf students.

Long train rides, strange hotels, meeting many new people—it all confused and frightened Helen. But Dr. Bell was very gentle. He sat her on his knees and guided her hands to his face. She felt his droopy mustache and heavy beard. Then he held his gold pocket watch against her cheek. She could feel the steady *tick-tock,* and she nodded her head in rhythm with it.

15

Helen was not afraid of this kind man. She sat still while he examined her. Then he told the Kellers, "I am certain that this clever little girl can be taught to communicate with others."

Dr. Bell suggested that Mr. Keller write to the Perkins Institute, where Laura Bridgman had learned the finger language. Perhaps the director, Michael Anagnos, could find the right teacher for Helen.

Mr. Keller did write the letter and soon received an answer. Mr. Anagnos knew of a young woman who would make a perfect teacher and companion for Helen. Her name was Annie Sullivan.

Arrangements were made quickly, and Annie Sullivan arrived in Tuscumbia on March 3, 1887. Mrs. Keller met her at the train, and they rode back to the house in a horse-drawn carriage.

Helen did not know why there was so much excitement in the house. But something told her that today was very special. When she could not find her mother anywhere, Helen went to the front door. She stood there and waited.

The carriage drew up in front of the house, and Annie Sullivan got her first look at Helen. The young girl's dress was dirty. Her light-brown curls were tangled and uncombed. She stood tense and frightened, like a startled fawn in the forest.

Mr. Keller helped Annie down from the carriage. She began to walk up the wooden steps to the front porch. Helen felt the vibrations made by the footsteps, and rushed at the stranger. Annie caught her before the wild charge knocked both of them down the steps.

Annie knelt and put her arms around Helen. She smiled as the child's fingers felt her eyes, her nose, her hair, and her hat. When Helen was finished "meeting" the stranger, Annie took her hand and they walked into the house, side by side.

Their first days together were not easy. Annie was unhappy about Helen's wild behavior. The child was allowed to walk around the dining table, sticking her fingers into everybody's food and taking whatever she wanted. She was very rough with Mildred, her baby sister, and with the dog, Belle. Helen would not let anybody comb her hair or wash her face and hands. And she would fly into a fierce rage when anyone tried to make her do something she didn't want to do.

Annie understood why Helen acted this way. Her parents felt so sorry for their unfortunate little girl that they could not bear to punish her, no matter what she did. They never made her obey rules.

Annie knew she had to tame this wild young girl. Helen had to learn to get along with other people. Until she did, she could not be taught anything.

First, Annie tried to win Helen's trust. She gave the little girl a doll that had been sent to Helen by the children at the Perkins Institute.

Helen ran her hands over the doll. She smiled and hugged it tightly. A moment later, Helen felt Annie take hold of her right hand. She felt fingers fluttering and tapping on her palm. The tapping stopped. Then again she felt the same tap-flutters on her palm. And again. Helen was puzzled.

Annie was using a special finger language to spell *d-o-l-l* in Helen's hand. She spelled it over and over. But Helen did not understand what was happening. Fear bubbled inside her. She threw the doll to the floor and rushed from the room.

Later that day, Annie took a piece of cake and touched Helen's hand to it. Helen loved cake and started to grab it. Annie stopped her. With one hand, she held Helen's left hand so that it just touched the cake. At the same time, she spelled *c-a-k-e* into Helen's right hand. She spelled it again and again.

Helen scowled. She started to pull away. Then, suddenly, she stopped. Putting her fingers in Annie's hand, she very slowly spelled *c-a-k-e*. Annie was thrilled with Helen's quick response. She gave Helen the cake. The young girl ate it happily.

As soon as Helen finished the last crumb, she felt Annie guide her left hand over the doll. Helen wanted it; it felt so soft and cuddly. She tugged at it. But Annie didn't let her have it. Then Helen put her fingers in Annie's hand and spelled *d-o-l*. Annie guided Helen's fingers through the second *l*, then placed the doll in Helen's arms. A smile spread across Helen's face.

This first success filled Annie with joy. Helen could learn! Now there was much to do. They began the next morning. Annie gave Helen milk and spelled *m-i-l-k* at the same time. She spelled *c-a-t*, while Helen petted the purring pet. And in this way, one new word followed another as the day flew by.

24

Although Annie's pupil showed great promise, there was still the problem of trying to discipline her. Sometimes Helen was very friendly. But at other times she had tantrums. She would kick and punch, shove people or throw things, until she got her way. Annie had to stop that. She knew that Mr. and Mrs. Keller never would. So she asked them to let her have complete control over Helen. They agreed.

At breakfast the next morning, Annie made Helen sit in her own chair at the table. She would not let the child take food from anyone else. The first time Helen tried to, Annie slapped her hand. Helen pinched Annie. Annie slapped her hand again. Helen stamped her feet in fury.

Annie dragged Helen to her own chair and made her sit in it. Then she put a spoon in the child's hand and guided it to her food-filled plate. Helen threw the spoon on the floor. Annie made her pick it up.

Mrs. Keller was crying, and Mr. Keller's face was a mask of pain. They hated to see their Helen suffer so. "She can't help herself," Mrs. Keller said. "She doesn't know better."

"We can help her to know better," Annie said in a gentle voice.

The Kellers left the dining room. Annie locked the door behind them. Then the battle really began. Annie was determined—Helen would learn to sit in her chair, eat properly, and fold her napkin when she was finished.

Helen walked around, touching every chair. When she found that her parents were gone, she crawled under the table. Annie pulled her out and sat her in her chair. Helen picked up the food with her fingers. Annie wiped them clean and gave her a spoon. Helen tried to drop it, but Annie wouldn't let her. Helen struggled. Annie was stronger.

Helen finally gave in and ate with the spoon. Even so, the battle was not over. When she finished eating, Helen tossed her napkin on the table. Annie made her pick it up, fold it, and place it beside her plate. A moment later, Helen flung the napkin to the floor. Annie made her get out of the chair, pick it up, and fold it again. Helen was sobbing, but she would not give in. Neither would Annie. At last, the napkin remained on the table, folded neatly. Only then did Annie unlock the door and let Helen out.

That night, Annie cried herself to sleep. She hated being harsh with Helen. She really loved the child, and wanted to be her friend. But first, she knew, Helen would have to depend on her. Only then could the real learning begin.

The battle of wills went on. But each day was a bit easier than the day before. One morning, Helen brought her comb to Annie for the first time. The next day, she let Annie get her ready for bed, then tuck her in for the night. And she was learning, too, to sew an apron for her doll, to crochet, to string beads, to "say" new words in finger talk.

Annie was delighted. At last, Helen liked her and trusted her. Yet there was something missing. Helen learned to make the words in finger talk, but she didn't *know* that they were words. She didn't know how to use them the way other people did.

Then, one day, Helen and Annie found the key that opened the door to the world for Helen Keller! It was April 5, 1887.

Annie described the moment of discovery in a letter to a friend. She wrote: "We went out to the pump house, and I made Helen hold her hands under the spout while I pumped. I spelled *w-a-t-e-r* into her free hand....The word coming so close upon the sensation of cold water rushing over her hand seemed to startle her. She dropped the mug and stood transfixed. A new light came into her face. She spelled *w-a-t-e-r* several times."

Then Helen reached down and touched the ground. Annie spelled *g-r-o-u-n-d* in her hand. Helen looked excited and pointed at Annie. Annie spelled *t-e-a-c-h-e-r*. Helen understood. And from that day on, she always called Annie Sullivan by the name, Teacher.

Now Helen pointed to herself. Annie spelled *H-e-l-e-n K-e-l-l-e-r*. Helen trembled with joy. She had a name, too!

31

Helen grabbed Annie's hand, and they flew into the house together. They found Mrs. Keller. Helen burrowed into her mother's arms, while Annie spelled *m-o-t-h-e-r* on her hand. Helen understood, and she nodded her head. Tears of thankfulness spilled from Mrs. Keller's eyes.

Helen couldn't learn enough to satisfy her thirst for words that day. She moved quickly around the house, touching things, learning the word for each one.

Years later, Helen wrote, "It was as if I had come back to life after being dead....Delicious sensations rippled through me, and strange sweet things that were locked up in my heart began to sing."

Helen was up with the sun the next morning, ready to learn more. She woke Annie with a hug and a kiss—and a tug of hands that said, "Hurry! Get up!"

It took a while for Helen to get dressed, but not because she made it a battle. As she put on each piece of clothing, she wanted to know all about it. Now she knew she wore a *dress*, and that it had *sleeves*, a *skirt*, *buttons*, *buttonholes*, a *collar*, a *belt*.

That was just the beginning. Words poured into Helen. She touched trees and grass and stones, and learned their names. She held an egg in her hand and felt a baby chick break through the shell and hatch. Then Annie's fingers told her all about the miracle of life she had felt.

Her teacher taught Helen to hop and skip and jump, telling her the word for each action. They did the same thing with foods, people's names, animals, flowers, furniture—everything in the world around them.

Annie wanted Helen to feel free and happy. So they spent most of their days outside, doing their lessons under a big tree in the garden. Helen learned geography by making maps with wet dirt. She shaped mountains and valleys, islands and rivers, even whole continents. She learned the shape of the Earth by holding an orange. Annie could hardly keep pace with Helen's endless desire for "more words."

If Helen could read, Annie decided, she would learn much faster. So Annie taught her to read braille. This is a way of printing words by using raised dots on paper. It was invented by Louis Braille in 1829, so that blind people could read by touch.

Annie had Helen feel the braille letter *a* with the fingers of one hand, while *a* was finger-spelled into her other hand. Then *b*... and *c*. Helen mastered the braille alphabet right away. Annie brought her books written in braille.

36

Helen loved them so much that she always slept with one in her bed.

Next, Annie taught Helen how to write in braille. Before long, Helen was writing stories, notes to Teacher, and letters to the blind children at the Perkins Institute.

Mr. and Mrs. Keller were thrilled at Helen's progress. "You have worked a miracle," Mr. Keller told Annie.

"The miracle is Helen," Annie insisted. "She can learn anything. Why, right now, we are working on ordinary writing. You will soon be reading her letters yourself."

Helen wanted to learn, learn, learn. Annie did her best, but she could see that Helen needed more than she could give her. So, in the spring of 1888, they took a train to Boston. There, at the Perkins Institute, Helen went to a real school for the first time.

Annie sat next to her in every class, spelling out the teacher's words in Helen's hand. Helen learned geography, zoology, Latin, German, arithmetic, English, Greek, and French. She didn't *have* to study all those subjects, she *wanted* to!

From eight o'clock in the morning until six o'clock at night, Helen went to classes. She stopped only for lunch and for an hour of play with other children in the gym. It was very tiring for Annie, who never left her side, but Helen thrived on it.

When Helen was ten, she read about a blind, deaf girl in Norway. That girl had learned to speak words out loud. Helen wanted to do the same thing. Annie took her to the Horace Mann School for the Deaf in Boston. There, a teacher named Sarah Fuller began working with Helen. First, Helen placed her hand on Miss Fuller's mouth. She felt the way words are formed. Then Helen tried to copy this with her mouth.

Helen could not hear her own voice, so she could not know if her words sounded the way they should. Annie worked with her, day and night. Their reward came when Helen said, "It is warm," in a clear voice. And when they went to Tuscumbia for summer vacation, Helen's family received a beautiful surprise.

The Kellers were waiting at the train station. Helen, prettier than ever, stepped down to the platform. Very proudly, she said, "Mother, I am not dumb now. Mildred, I love you. Father, I am glad to be home."

This was a moment the Kellers would never forget.

It was a wonderful summer vacation. Then Helen and Annie returned to school in Boston. And this is how they spent each year as Helen grew into her teens.

One day, Helen told Annie of a new goal she had her heart set on. She wanted to go to college. Some of her friends felt college would be too hard for Helen, and that she would be crushed by failure. But Helen refused to give up her dream.

She studied tirelessly for the entrance examinations. Her hand printing was slow, so Helen learned to use a typewriter. And she typed her answers through a nine-hour preliminary exam, plus a full-day final exam.

Helen did brilliantly. She won honors in English and German and was given credit in advanced Latin. Now her friends *had* to believe in her dream!

Helen attended Radcliffe College in the fall of 1900. During her four years there, she found her life's work: to help others. She would tell the world her story. She would show everyone that the deaf and the blind can learn. Helen wanted to bring hope to the handicapped. Her life was proof that everyone deserved a chance to learn.

In the years that followed, Helen wrote many books and magazine articles. She traveled around the world, speaking to people of all nations. Until Annie died, in 1936, she was with Helen every step of the way. Polly Thompson, a young Scottish woman, took Annie's place at Helen's side. And together they carried on Helen's work.

During World War II, Helen visited soldiers who had been blinded in battle. She gave them courage and faith in the future. After the war, she worked with blind and deaf children. "I cannot stop to grow old while there is so much work to do," she said, "and so many children to help."

Until her death, on June 1, 1968, this most remarkable woman continued to give love, hope, and inspiration to thousands of human beings.

Index

47

The Courage of Helen Keller

by Francene Sabin
illustrated by Jean Meyer

This edition published 1998 by Troll Communications L.L.C.

Printed in the United States of America.

10   9   8   7   6

Cover art by Shi Chen.

Library of Congress Cataloging-in-Publication Data

Sabin, Francene.
    Courage of Helen Keller.

    Summary: Recounts how the young Helen Keller, left blind and
deaf by a childhood illness, learned to communicate with the world.
    1. Keller, Helen, 1880-1968—Juvenile literature. 2. Blind-deaf—
United States—Biography—Juvenile literature. [1. Keller, Helen, 1880-1968.
2. Blind.   3. Deaf.   4. Physically handicapped]   I. Meyer, Jean, ill.
II. Title.
HV1624.K4S25   362.4'1'0924 [B] [92]   81-23109
    ISBN 0-89375-754-3 (lib. bdg.)   AACR2
    ISBN 0-8167-4559-5 (pbk.)